Awesome Facts about

Bugs

Claire Llewellyn

Aladdin / Watts
London • Sydney

Contents

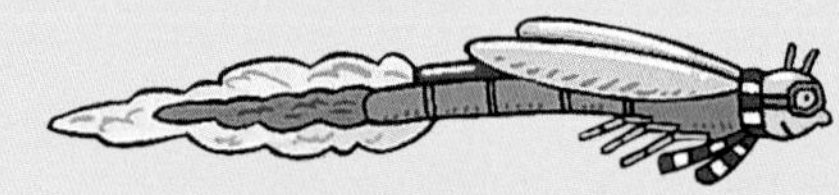

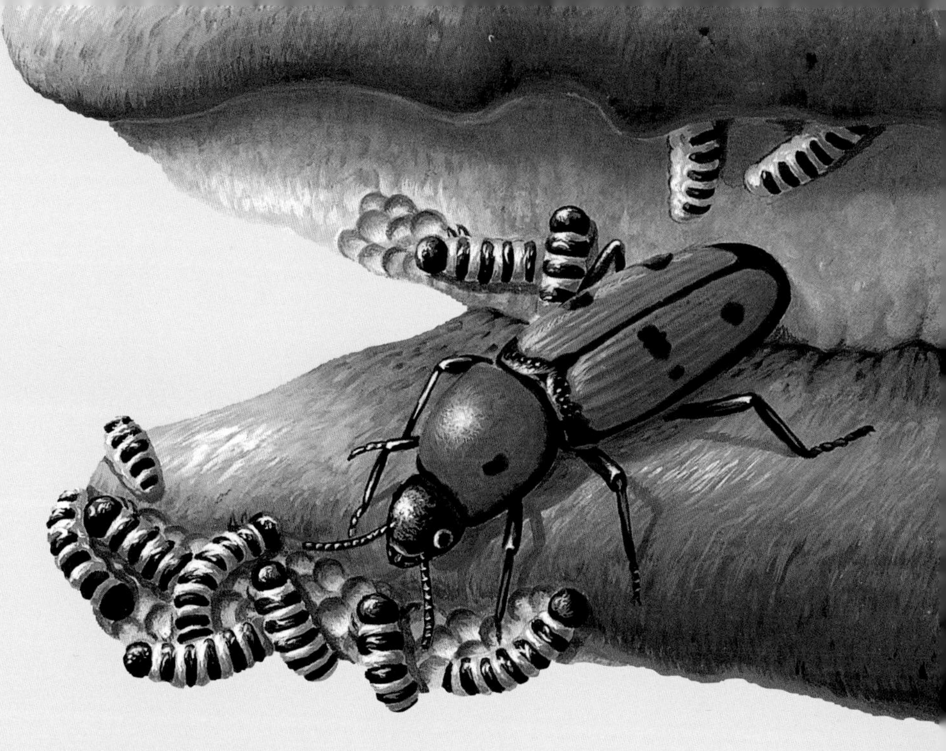

Introduction

Did *you* know that you would need to use dynamite to blow up a termite's home?
... that stick insects can grow as long as a cat?
... that some wasps lay their eggs in pots?

Discover for yourself amazing facts about the insect world, from the tiniest fairy fly and the high-jumping flea to the insect that eats birds...

Look out for this symbol which means there is a fun project for you to try.

Is it true or is it false? Watch for this symbol and try to answer the question before reading on for the answer.

Don't forget to check the borders for extra amazing facts.

Three pairs of legs

All insects have six legs. Counting the legs is a sure way of identifying an insect. Woodlice, spiders, mites and centipedes aren't insects – they have far too many legs.

Goliath beetle

An insect has three different parts to its body: the head, the *thorax* and the *abdomen*. A hard outer skeleton makes the insect waterproof and protects its soft insides.

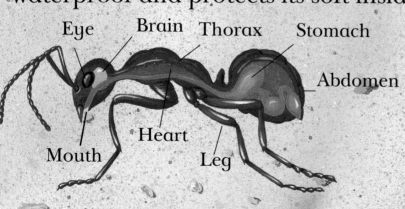

Eye
Brain
Thorax
Stomach
Abdomen
Mouth
Heart
Leg

Woodlouse

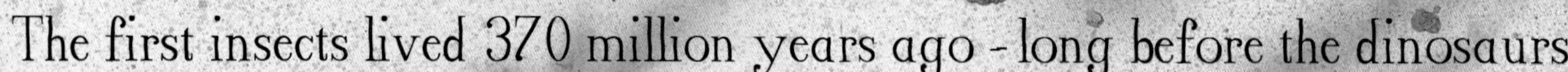

The first insects lived 370 million years ago - long before the dinosaurs.

Bad news: There are about 280,000 kinds of wasps, bees and ants.

SEARCH & FIND SEARCH & FIND
Find one insect and three imposters.
Centipede
Bird-eating spider

People who study insects are called entomologists. They learn about insects, how and where they live and how best to protect them.

There are well over a million kinds of insects in the world. That's more than all the other kinds of animals put together! Entomologists discover 8,000 new insects every year.

Dragonflies are sprinters. In short bursts they zoom along at over 50 km/h.

Beetle
A wasp's second pair of wings is hard to see.
Wasp
Bluebottle
SEARCH & FIND
Can you find five true flies?
SEARCH & FIND

True or false?

Flies have only one pair of wings.

Answer: **True**

Flies that have one pair of wings, such as the housefly, are called true flies. Dragonflies and mayflies have two pairs of wings, so they're not true flies at all. *Beetles* have one pair of wings but their *wingcases* count as a second pair – so beetles are not true flies either!

Flying beetles

Beetles can fly when they need to. They open up their wingcases, unfold their soft wings and take off!

Flying insects survive tropical storms because the raindrops make a breeze as they fall, which blows tiny insects aside. They end up flying between the drops.

A butterfly's wings are covered with rows of scales, arranged like the tiles on a roof. Each scale is like a tiny speck of dust.

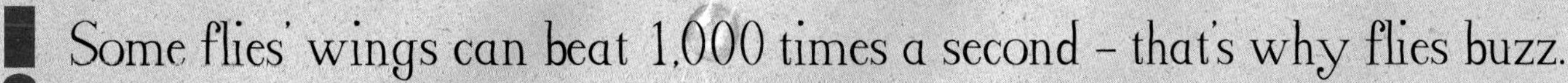

! Some flies' wings can beat 1,000 times a second – that's why flies buzz.

How butterflies grow

Like many insects, butterflies grow by changing completely – from an egg, to a *caterpillar*, to a *pupa*, to a butterfly. This change is called *metamorphosis.*

The Austrian writer Franz Kafka, wrote a book called Metamorphosis. It's about a man who changed into a giant insect.

SEARCH & FIND SEARCH & FIND

Can you find nine caterpillars?

Not all insects change as they grow. Baby shield bugs look like their parents when they hatch. They just get bigger and bigger, and eventually grow their wings.

Mayflies spend most of their lives as wingless *larvae*. Once they change into adult mayflies, they only live for a day.

Walking on water

SEARCH & FIND
Can you find the water snail?
SEARCH & FIND

Some bugs can walk on water. Pondskaters are so light they can skim across ponds without falling in. Hairy tufts on their tiny feet help them to stay afloat.

Dragonflies begin life in water as creatures called *nymphs*. They will attack small fish and tadpoles that are bigger than themselves.

! A water boatman lies on its back and rows through the water.

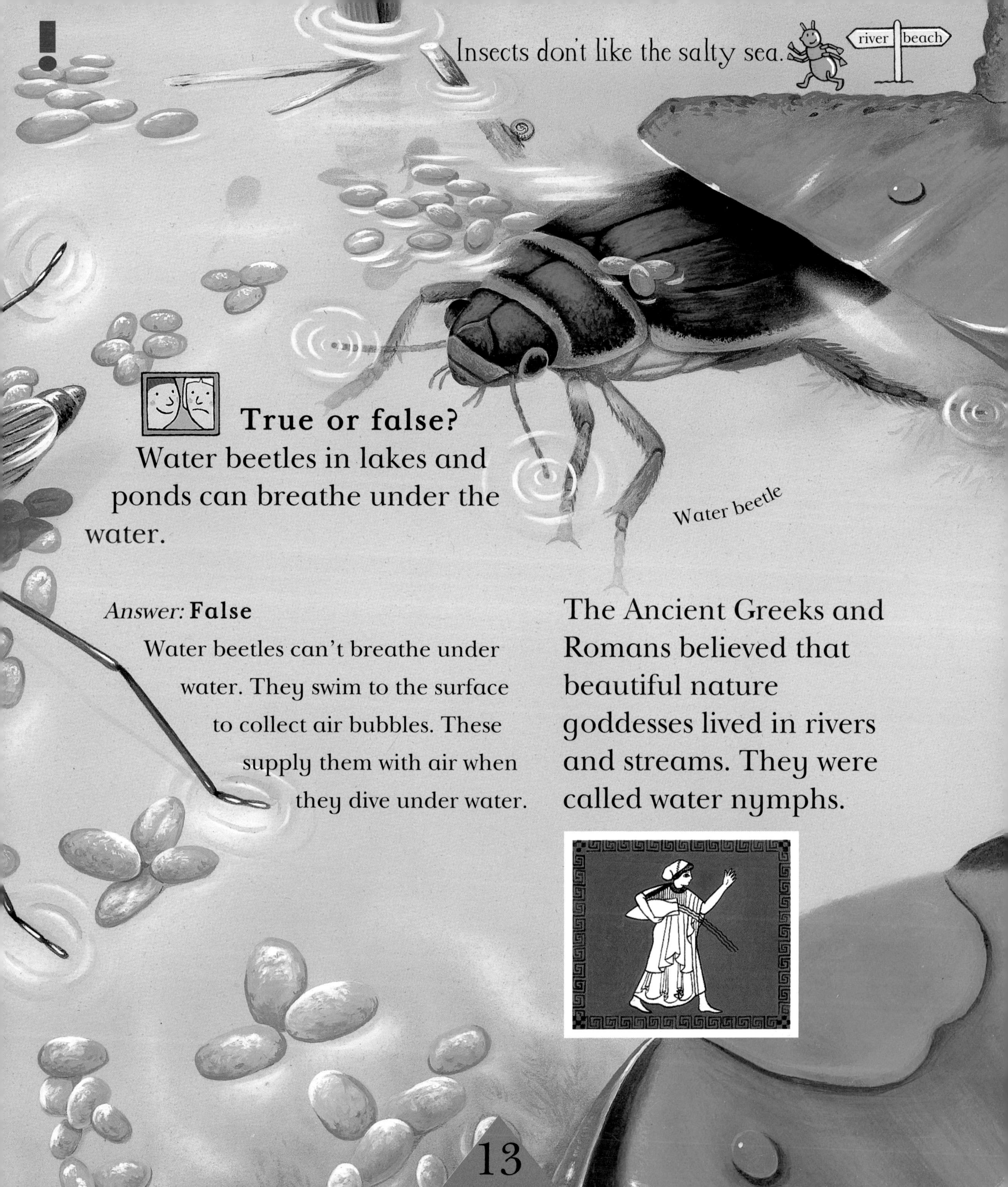

True or false?
Water beetles in lakes and ponds can breathe under the water.

Answer: **False**
Water beetles can't breathe under water. They swim to the surface to collect air bubbles. These supply them with air when they dive under water.

The Ancient Greeks and Romans believed that beautiful nature goddesses lived in rivers and streams. They were called water nymphs.

Air-conditioning

Termites build themselves tall mud towers to live in. Each tower has a chimney which draws up warm air and keeps the nest cool. A bit like a house with air-conditioning.

Tropical weaver ants build their homes out of leaves. Some of the ants hold the leaves together, while others stick them with a sticky glue. The glue comes from larvae the ants carry in their jaws.

SEARCH & FIND

Can you find the *queen* termite?

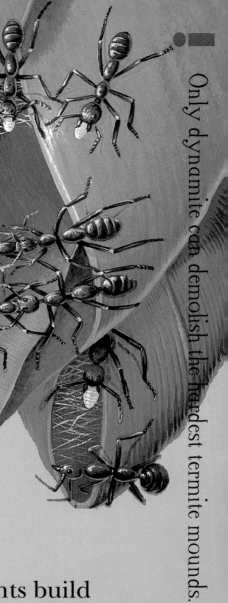

Only dynamite can demolish the hardest termite mounds.

1. Chimney
2. Food store
3. Queen's chamber
4. Larvae galleries

True or false?
Some insects live in tents in the trees.

Answer: **True**
Some caterpillars spin a huge silk canopy around their branch, and stay safe and sound inside.

Insects that live together are called social insects. Ants, termites, bees and wasps are all social insects, and live in large groups called colonies. This is the best way for them to survive.

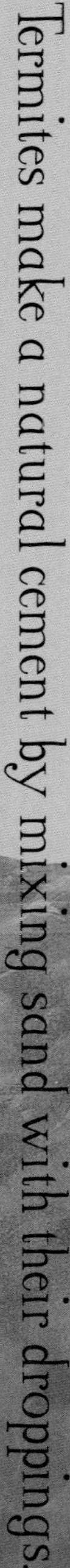

Termites make a natural cement by mixing sand with their droppings.

Potter wasp

Making mud pots

The female potter wasp makes tiny mud pots to lay each of her eggs in. Before sealing a pot, she pokes a *grub* inside – a meal for her young when it hatches.

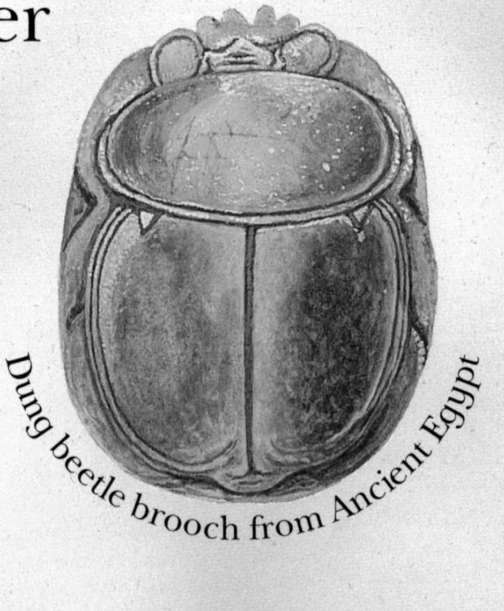

In Ancient Egypt, the dung beetle was the symbol for the Sun god, who rolled the Sun across the sky each day.

Dung beetle brooch from Ancient Egypt

! Most insects don't make nests. They just lay their eggs near some food.

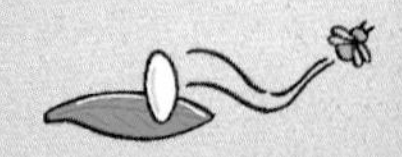

True or false?

Insects make bad parents. They never look after their young.

Answer: **False**

The female fungus beetle cleans and protects her eggs until they hatch. Then she helps the larvae to feed for about two weeks.

Fungus beetle

You can make a giant potter wasp's pot. Roll damp clay into thin ropes, and coil them in circles to make a jar. Copy the shape from the picture (above left). Be sure to make a lip around the top. Smooth the sides and leave it to dry.

Dung beetles lay their eggs inside balls of dung – their larvae's favourite food. The beetles make the balls by rolling bits of dung along the ground.

True or false?

A honey bee tastes its food with its feet.

Answer: **True**

A honey bee tastes with its feet as well as its mouth. It can sample its food as soon as it lands on it. So can houseflies.

Butterflies suck up the *nectar* from flowers through a long tongue called a proboscis. When they're not feeding, they keep it curled up out of the way.

! Cockroaches eat anything – meat, bread, fruit, cardboard...

Honeypot ants store nectar in their bodies for others to feed on.

Farming ants

Just as farmers keep cows, some ants keep *aphids*. They protect them from their enemies, and in return the ants 'milk' the aphids for honeydew, which they suck up.

If you want to study moths you can attract them by leaving a mixture of sugar and water near a lighted, open window at night.

SEARCH & FIND

Can you find the bumble bee?

SEARCH & FIND

Lizards for lunch

The praying mantis is a fierce hunter. When it snaps its spiny legs, its helpless prey is trapped inside. Most praying mantises eat other insects, but some catch lizards and frogs.

! Kissing bugs bite people's faces and suck up their blood.

SEARCH & FIND SEARCH & FIND

Can you find the praying mantis' meal?

Some tropical moths feed on the salty tears of horses and deer. The moths flutter around the animals' eyes to make them cry!

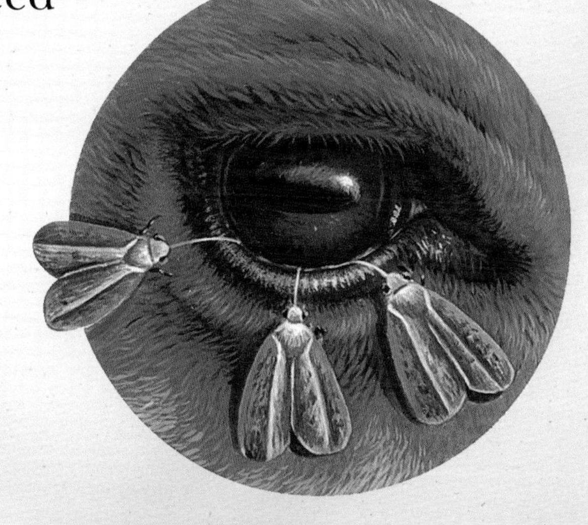

Mosquito

When the assassin bug catches a tasty meal, it injects it with poison. This turns the prey's body to soup. Then the bug sucks it all up.

Not all mosquitos suck up blood. Only the females do. They need blood to make their eggs. Male mosquitos feed on nectar.

Assassin bug

! Stick insects change their colour as they move from plant to plant.

Camouflage

Some leaves are insects in disguise. Leaf insects blend in so well with the leaves on which they feed that they're nearly invisible. This way of hiding is called *camouflage*.

Many animals eat caterpillars, but the hawkmoth caterpillar has a clever disguise to frighten its enemies away. It looks just like a hungry snake!

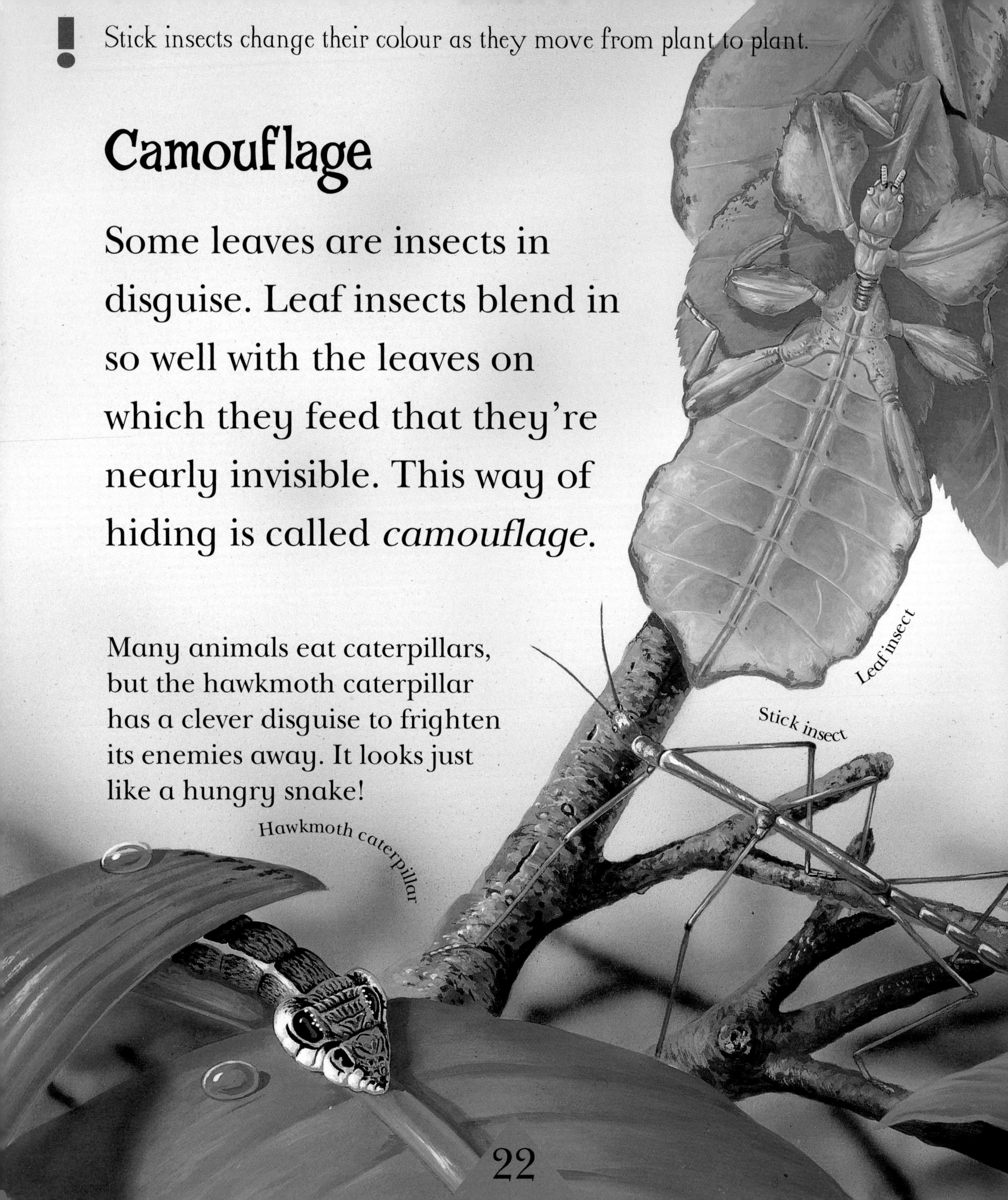

These fly orchids aren't insects at all but plants that mimic insects. They look like female insects. This attracts the male insects to them which can then pollinate (fertilise) them.

Camouflage isn't only for defence. The pink flower mantis is brilliantly hidden inside an orchid – the better to ambush its prey.

When thorn bugs land on twigs, they look like nasty prickles. And even if they're caught, they're much too sharp to eat.

Bugs that stink

Stink bugs can give off a terrible stink! When they are frightened, they let out a strong smell from tiny holes between their legs. This gets rid of enemies – fast!

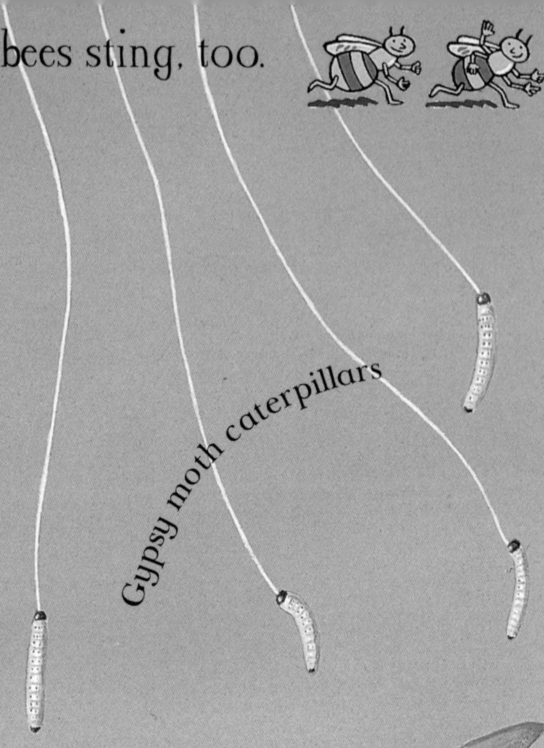

Gypsy moth caterpillars

Gypsy moth caterpillars escape danger by dropping down on a line of silk and wafting away on the wind.

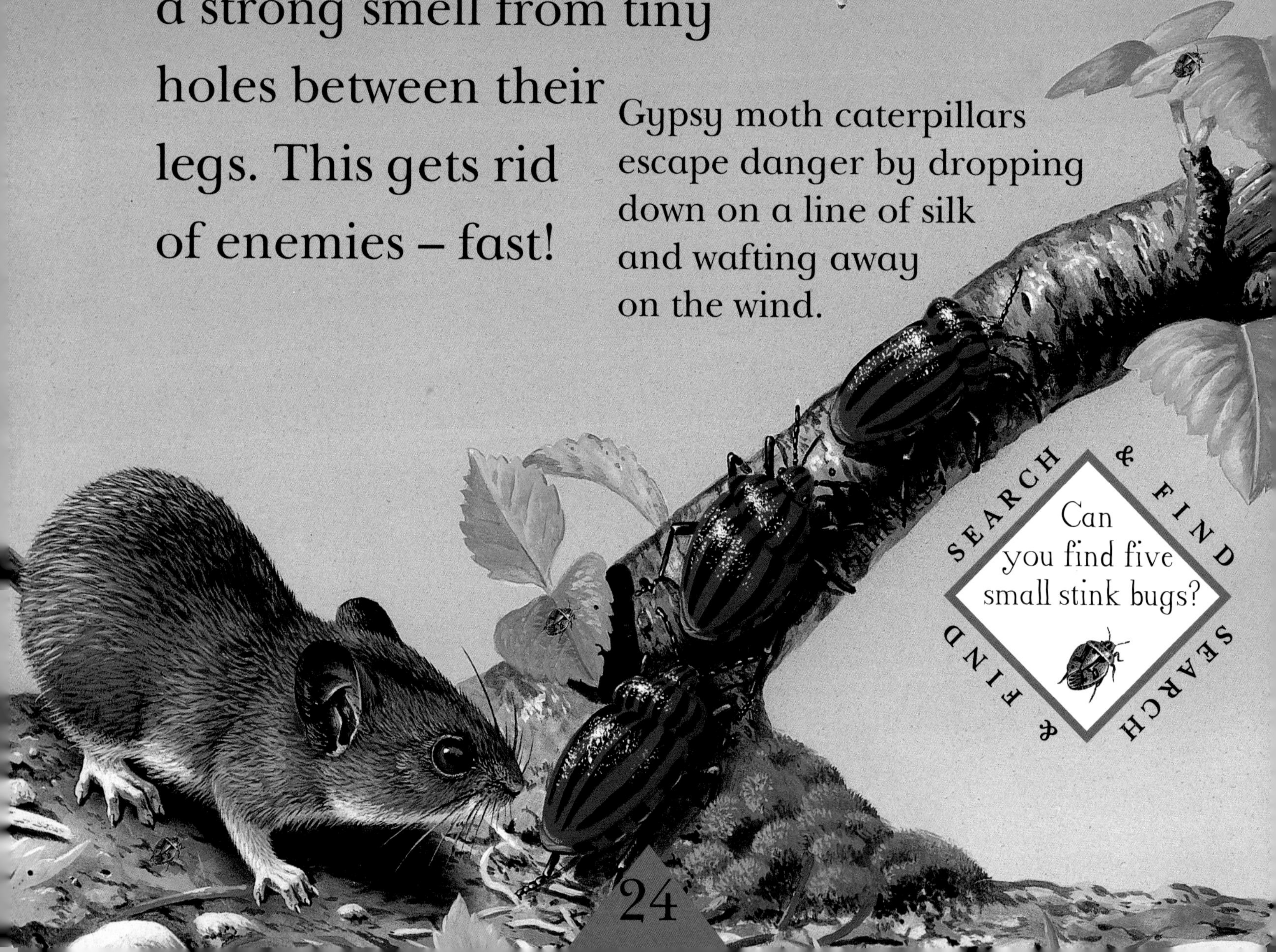

SEARCH & FIND

Can you find five small stink bugs?

The wetapunga is a huge *cricket* with long legs covered in spikes. When it's caught by a bird, the weta kicks out for all it's worth, and is usually dropped in surprise!

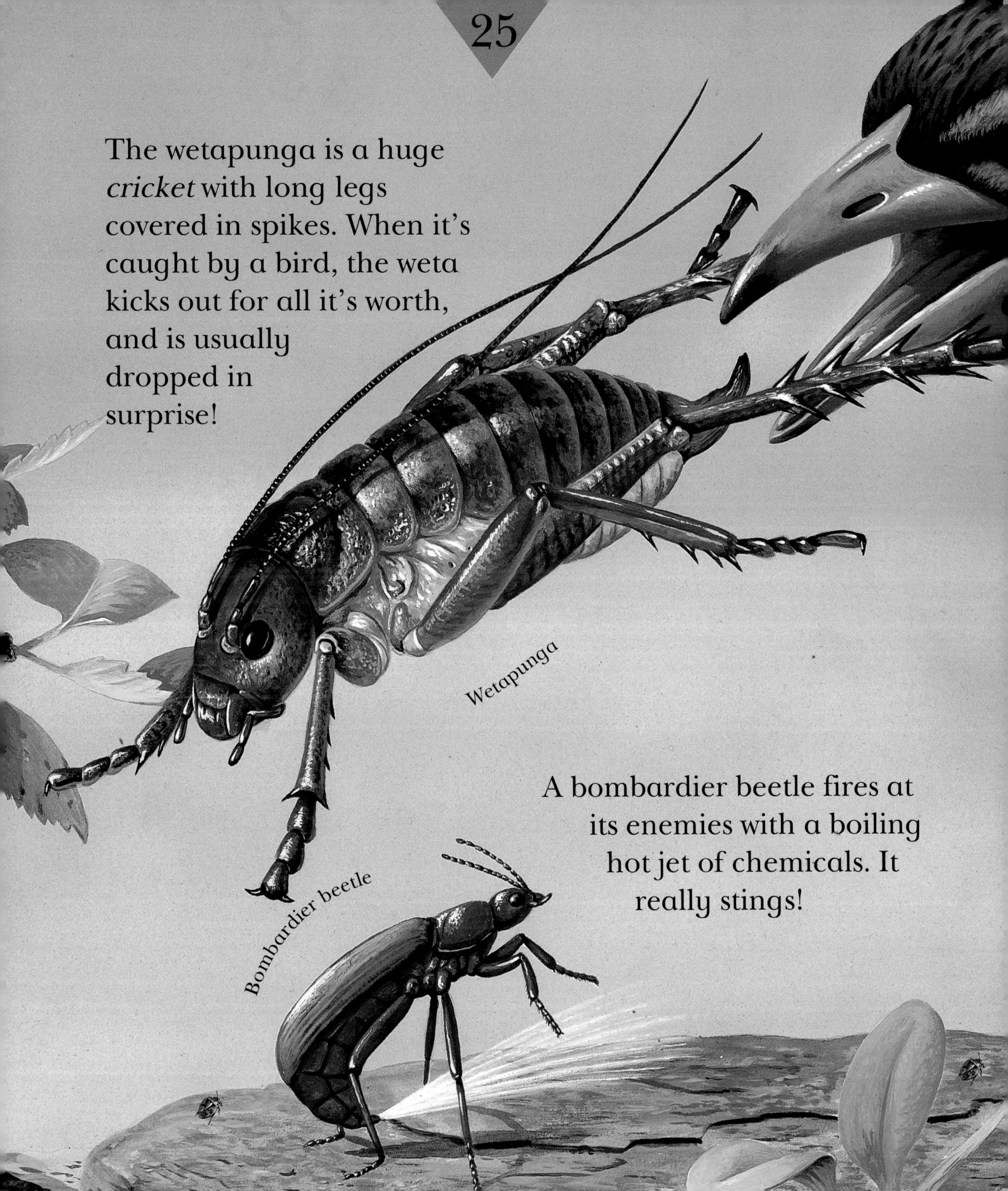

A bombardier beetle fires at its enemies with a boiling hot jet of chemicals. It really stings!

True or false?

You could read by the light of a glow-worm.

Answer: **True**
Glow-worms were once used as reading lamps. Their glow lasts two hours or more.

Bugs that glow

To find a mate, female fireflies make a light in their abdomen and flash signals to males. They are also known as glow-worms.

! When two ants meet, they often touch feelers in greeting.

Male staghorn beetles fight with each other for a female.

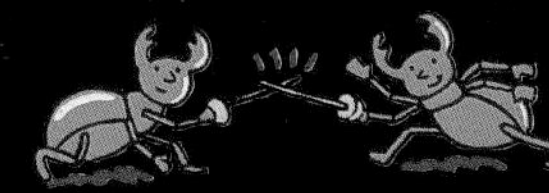

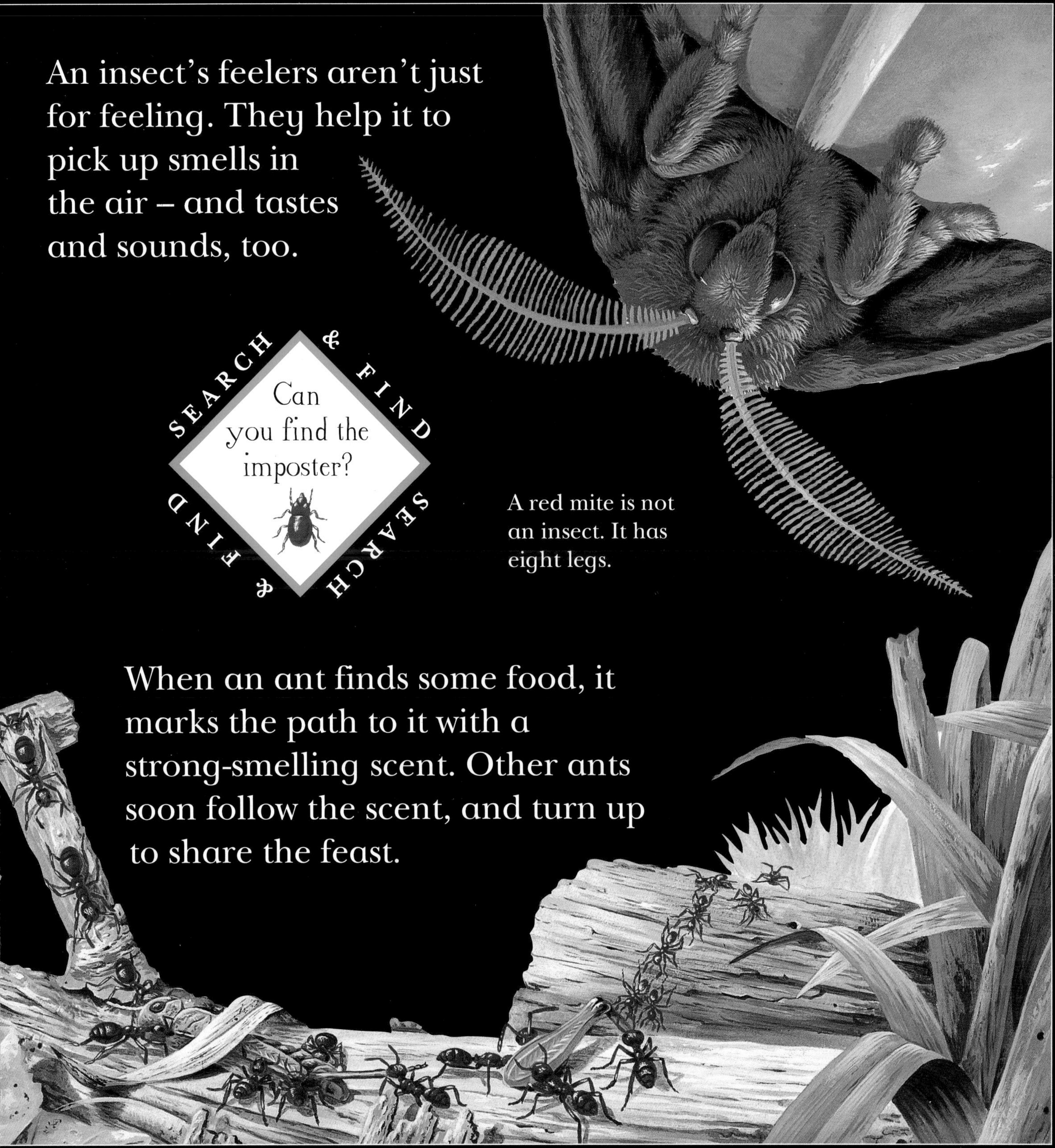

An insect's feelers aren't just for feeling. They help it to pick up smells in the air – and tastes and sounds, too.

SEARCH & FIND SEARCH & FIND

Can you find the imposter?

A red mite is not an insect. It has eight legs.

When an ant finds some food, it marks the path to it with a strong-smelling scent. Other ants soon follow the scent, and turn up to share the feast.

500 years ago, rat fleas were the most dangerous insects in the world. They spread a deadly sickness called the plague, which killed millions and millions of people.

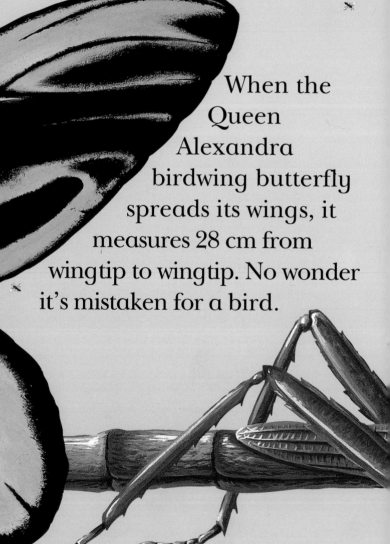

When the Queen Alexandra birdwing butterfly spreads its wings, it measures 28 cm from wingtip to wingtip. No wonder it's mistaken for a bird.

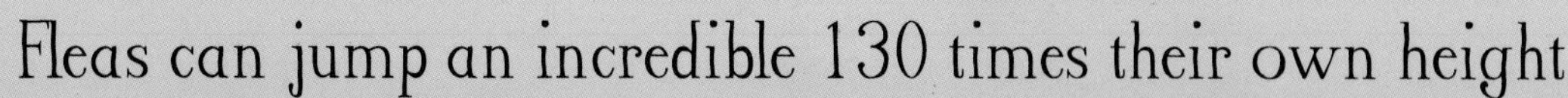

Fleas can jump an incredible 130 times their own height.

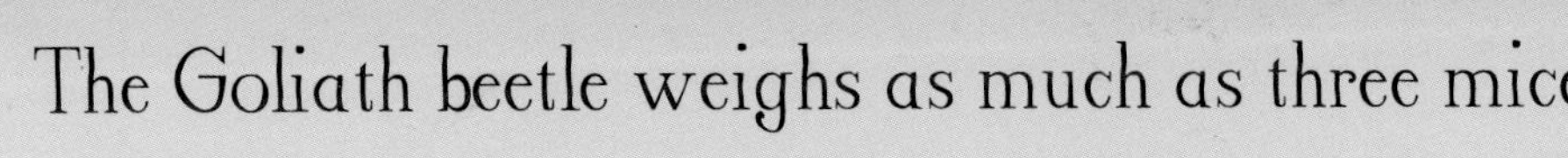

Insect giant

The biggest insect in the world is the stick insect. The Indonesian giant stick insect is over 30 cm long.

It's difficult to see real fairy flies – they are the size of a pinprick.

Male cicadas are the loudest insects in the world. Their clicking noise can be heard by females a kilometre away.

SEARCH & FIND

Can you find ten fairy flies?

SEARCH & FIND

Glossary

Abdomen
The last of the three parts of an insect's body.

Aphids
Tiny insects, such as greenflies, that feed by sucking up the juices from plants.

Beetles
A group of insects that have hard wingcases and can usually fly.

Camouflage
The colours and markings on an insect which help it to blend in with its surroundings and make it difficult to see.

Caterpillar
The larva of a moth or butterfly.

Crickets
A group of insects that are related to grasshoppers, and make a loud chirping noise.

Grub
The young caterpillar-like stage of a beetle and some other insects.

Larva (*plural*: larvae)
The young stage of an insect before metamorphosis. Caterpillars, maggots and grubs are all types of larvae.

Metamorphosis
The change from the young stage to the adult stage of an insect. Many insects change from a larva, to a pupa, to a fully-grown adult.

Nectar
The sweet liquid inside flowers, which attracts insects and other animals.

Nymph
The young stage of an insect that hatches looking just like its parents.

Pupa
The stage in an insect's life when it develops inside a hard, protective case.

Queen
The only egg-laying female in a nest of social insects, such as termites and bees.

Thorax
The middle part of an insect's body, between the head and the abdomen.

Wingcases
Hard outer wings that are not used for flying.

Index